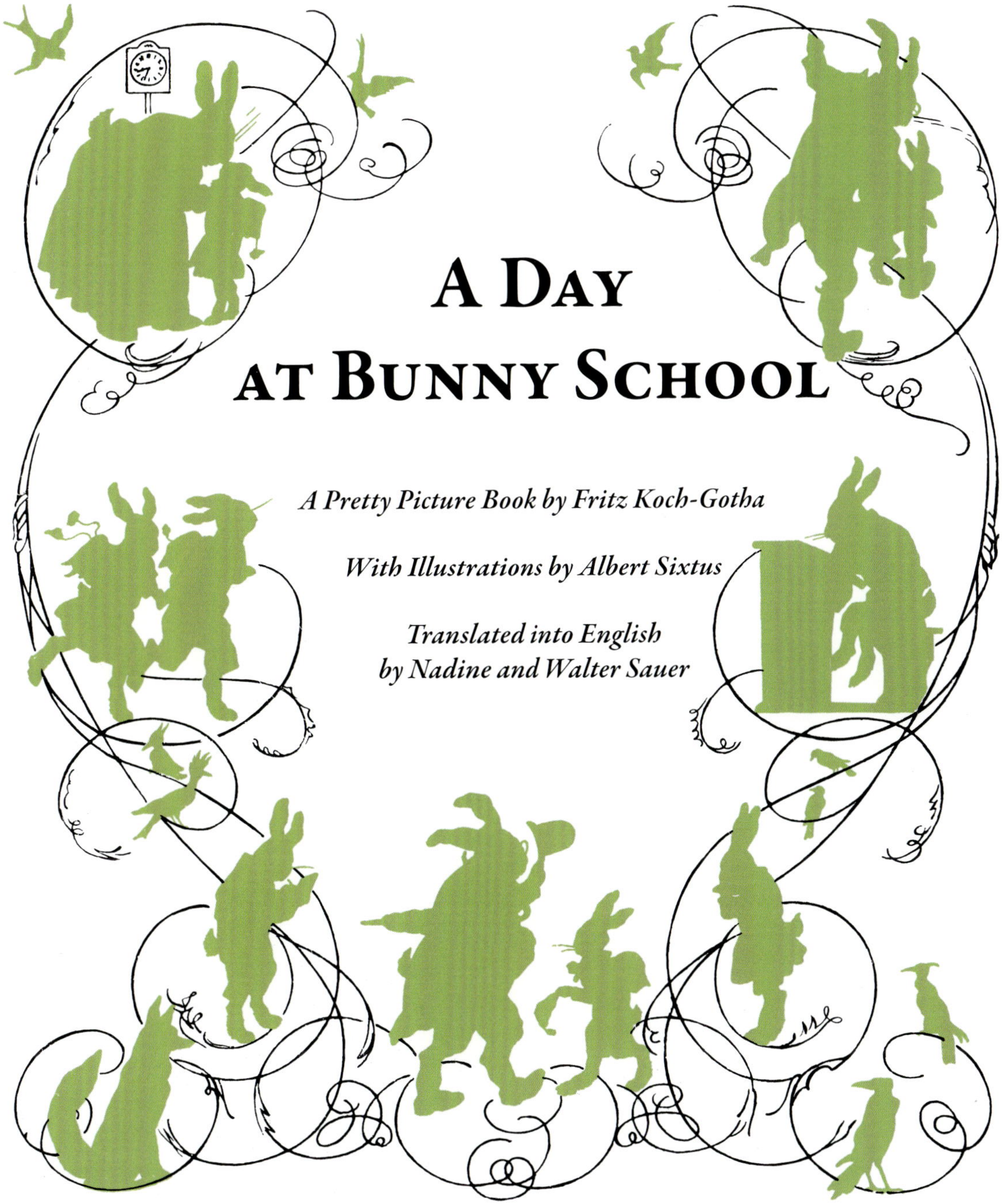

A Day at Bunny School

A Pretty Picture Book by Fritz Koch-Gotha

With Illustrations by Albert Sixtus

Translated into English by Nadine and Walter Sauer

"Children," Mother Rabbit said,
"Blow your noses, go ahead
Use this cabbage leaf, and then
Don't forget book, slate and pen.
Wet your sponges, and I mean,
Are your pawses nice and clean?"
"Yes." – "Now off to school you go."
"Bye-bye Mummy, cheerio."

»Kinder«, spricht die Mutter Hase,
»putzt euch noch einmal die Nase
mit dem Kohlblatt-Taschentuch!
Nehmt nun Tafel, Stift und Buch!
Tunkt auch eure Schwämmchen ein!
Sind denn eure Pfötchen rein?
»Ja!« – »Nun marsch, zur Schule gehn!«
»Mütterchen, auf Wiedersehn!«

F. Koch-Gotha - 23

Bunny Jack and bunny Jane –
See them walking down the lane,
Paw in paw, they're on their way,
Almost six, no time to play.
Other little rabbits are
Joining them from near and far,
Satchels shouldered everyone
There with bobbing tails they run.

Hasenhans und Hasengretchen
gehen lustig Pfot' in Pfötchen
um die sechste Morgenstund'
durch den bunten Wiesengrund.
Viele andre Hasenjungen
kommen schnell herbeigesprungen.
Auf dem Rücken sitzt das Ränzchen,
hinten wippt das Hasenschwänzchen.

O'er the brook, just one more hop,
At the schoolyard they all stop.
Where the highest fir trees grow
Little desks stand row by row,
Nicely placed in twos and threes
In the clearing by the trees.
Hoppity-hop – then Jack and Jane
Find their places there again.

Hops, noch über diese Quelle!
Hei, sie sind an Ort und Stelle!
Wo die hohen Tannen stehn,
kann man eine Wiese sehn.
Kleine Bänke stehn in Reihen,
hier zu zweien, da zu dreien.
Hopphopphopp, noch einen Satz,
und sie sind auf ihrem Platz.

Now the schoolbell rings – ding-dong –
Through the meadow loud and long,
Till the teacher has appeared –
Rounded glasses, greying beard,
Ears well-groomed in rabbit fashion –
Teaching is his greatest passion.
Every bunny bows its head
While the morning prayer is said.

Hausmann mit dem bunten Rocke
läutet hell die Morgenglocke,
und beim letzten Glockenton
kommt der alte Lehrer schon:
Runde Brille, grauer Bart,
Ohren lang nach Hasenart.
Artig faltet man die Hände,
bis das Frühgebet zu Ende.

Lesson one is botany.
Bunnies study carefully
Tasty herbs and plants to eat,
What is sour, what is sweet.
They must raise their paws to show
Class and teacher what they know.
Jack, who's quicker than the rest,
Knows that cabbage tastes the best.

Nun beginnt die erste Stunde,
Häschen haben Pflanzenkunde.
Eh' sie eine Antwort geben,
müssen sie die Pfötchen heben.
Und der Lehrer fragt geschwind,
welche Kräuter eßbar sind.
Hasenhans, der weiß das wohl:
»Am allerbesten schmeckt der Kohl!«

Lesson two, and bunnies hear of
Animals they live in fear of.
Stories told and stories read
Fill the bunnies all with dread
Of the fox, their foe so sly,
How he prowls through woods nearby.
Jane can only hope and pray
Not to meet the fox one day.

In der nächsten Stunde dann
kommt die Tiergeschichte dran.
Von dem alten Fuchs, dem bösen,
wird erzählt und vorgelesen,
wie er leise, husch, husch, husch,
schleicht durch Wiese, Feld und Busch.
Und die kleine Gretel denkt:
»Wenn er mich nur nicht mal fängt!«

Der Fuchs
Der Rotfuchs
Der Rotfuchs wohnt in
einer Höhle im tiefen Wald
Er ist ein großer Räuber
Er hat scharfe spitze
Zähne. Wehe euch,
wenn er euch packt!
Er ißt gern Hühner,
und Gänsebraten oder
am liebsten sticht er
doch ein Häschen auf
einen Tisch. Dann

See how bunny eyes now shine
As they colour eggs so fine.
Each has got a brush in hand,
Painting them quite gaily, and
All the eggs once brown or white
Gleam and glow in colours bright.
Hours of practice, years of habit,
Make a future Easter rabbit.

Seht, wie ihre Augen strahlen,
wenn sie lernen Eier malen!
Jedes Häslein nimmt gewandt
einen Pinsel in die Hand,
färbt die Eier, weiß und rund,
mit den schönsten Farben bunt.
Wer's nicht kann, der darf auf Erden
nie ein Osterhase werden.

When the school break starts at eight
All the pupils cannot wait.
Bunny boys run down to play
In the meadow straight away,
While the girls all nice and quiet
Nibble on their cabbage diet,
Strolling, chatting with their friends
Till the morning break then ends.

Wenn die Pause nun beginnt,
geht's zur Wiese wie der Wind.
Lustig sind die Hasenjungen,
toll wird da herumgesprungen.
Doch die Mädchen knabbern stumm
an dem Frühstückskraut herum,
und sie wandern, tipp-tipp-tapp,
mit der Freundin auf und ab.

Bunny Max, that little squirt,
Broke a bench, tore Lizzie's skirt,
Hadn't learnt his lines by heart,
Was a nuisance from the start,
Laughed and didn't mind his teacher.
Shame on you, you naughty creature.
To the corner he is sent,
Standing there his punishment.

Hasenmax, der Bösewicht,
konnte heut sein Verschen nicht,
hat gepfiffen und geschwätzt,
Hasenlieschens Rock zerfetzt,
eine neue Bank zerkracht
und dabei noch laut gelacht.
In die Ecke muß er nun.
Ei, da kann er Buße tun!

F Koch-Gotha

Best in class, sweet Carolin,
Brings the teacher's violin,
Which he tunes g-d-a-e,
Each string one by one, then he
Puts some rosin on his bow,
Plays a tune all bunnies know.
Many rabbit songs ring out
Through the forest round about.

Klassenerste, Hasenmine,
holt des Lehrers Violine,
der den Bogen rasch und leicht
mit dem gelben Harz bestreicht.
Ping-pang-pung! – Die Geige stimmt,
hoch er sie zum Halse nimmt.
Durch die Sommerlüfte zieht
manch ein schönes Hasenlied.

With a watering can of green
Bunny boys can now be seen
Sprinkling cabbage in their beds,
Since they're dry and hang their heads.
And the bunny girls with care
Weed between the lettuce there.
See, their teacher stays in sight,
Watching that they do it right.

Mit den grünen Wasserkännchen
laufen hier die Hasenmännchen,
weil das Kraut die Blätter hängt,
wird's mit kühlem Naß besprengt.
Mädchen hocken vor den Beeten,
um das Unkraut auszujäten.
Und der Lehrer, der gibt acht,
daß es jeder richtig macht.

F Koch-Gotha

Sports is last. Here bunnies learn
How to skip and jump and turn –
Forwards, sideways, and to dive –
Tricks they need to stay alive
And avoid the hunter's gun
And his wicked hound outrun,
Laughing boldly in his face
And survive the winter chase.

In der allerletzten Stunde
turnen sie im Waldesgrunde.
Und sie lernen wie beim Jagen
man durch flinkes Hakenschlagen
kann dem Hund 'ne Nase drehn
und dem sichern Tod entgehn,
wenn im Winter durch den Wald
laut des Jägers Büchse knallt.

F. Koch-Gotha -23

Teacher says, "Now bunnies dear,
Pack your things and line up here
Two by two, then off for home,
From the pathway do not roam.
Never stray through underbrush,
Careful now, remember – hush!
Once the fox gets hold of you
There is nothing you can do."

Endlich spricht der Lehrersmann:
»Liebe Häschen, tretet an!
Laßt nichts in der Schule liegen!
Auf dem Heimweg – stillgeschwiegen!
Nicht vom Wege seitwärts springen!
Nicht in dunkle Büsche dringen!
Hat der Rotfuchs euch am Kragen,
hilft kein Betteln, hilft kein Klagen.«

Listen there, who is that crying?
"Dearest bunnies, I am dying,
Bring me leaves, I am so weak
And so ill, can hardly speak."
'Tis the fox with flashing eyes
Telling bunnies cruel lies.
Hopping here and hopping there,
Bunnies scatter everywhere.

Horch, wer wimmert dort so sehr:
»Liebe Häschen, kommt mal her!
Ach, ich bin so schwach und matt!
Bringt mir doch ein frisches Blatt!«
Huhuhu! – Es ist der Fuchs!
Augen leuchten wie beim Luchs.
Hopsa – hopsa, wie der Wind
rennt ein jedes Hasenkind!

School is out. The bunnies are
Safely home with Ma and Pa.
Dinner's on the table soon
And they eat it with a spoon –
Water-cress and cabbage hot –
Mother serves it from a pot.
If I weren't a child so blessed
Bunnydom would please me best.

So – nun ist die Schule aus,
und die Häschen sind zu Haus,
setzen hungrig sich zu Tisch,
greifen nach dem Löffel frisch:
Kohlgemüse, Kressenblatt,
ei, da essen sie sich satt!
Wär' ich nicht ein Kindelein,
möcht' ich gleich ein Häschen sein!

F. Koch-Gotha -29-

Titel der deutschen Originalausgabe: Die Häschenschule. Ein lustiges Bilderbuch
von Fritz Koch-Gotha zu Versen von Albert Sixtus.

Esslinger Verlag J. F. Schreiber GmbH, Esslingen
www.esslinger-verlag.de

For Audrey

Genehmigte Lizenzausgabe für:

69239 Neckarsteinach
www.verlag-tintenfass.de
info@verlag-tintenfass.de

Satz: Philipp J. Sauer

FSC
www.fsc.org
MIX
Papier aus verantwortungsvollen Quellen
FSC® C101807

ISBN 978-3-943052-27-5